SURVIVAL ON THE SLOPES

WINA STURGEON

Illustrations by
GARY PATTERSON

A THOUGHT FACTORY BOOK

CONTEMPORARY BOOKS, INC.
CHICAGO

Library of Congress Cataloging-in-Publication Data

Sturgeon, Wina, 1942–
   Survival on the slopes.

   "A Thought Factory book."
   1. Skis and skiing—Anecdotes, facetiae, satire,
etc.   I. Patterson, Gary.   II. Title.
PN6231.S549S7   1985   818'.5402   85-25529
ISBN 0-8092-5132-9 (pbk.)

Copyright © 1985 by Wina Sturgeon
Illustrations © 1985 by Thought Factory

All rights reserved. No part of this book may be reproduced in any form without permission in writing from the publisher, except by a reviewer who may quote brief passages in a review to be printed in a magazine or newspaper.

Published by Contemporary Books, Inc.
180 North Michigan Avenue, Chicago, Illinois 60601
Manufactured in the United States of America
Library of Congress Catalog Number: 85-25529
International Standard Book Number: 0-8092-5234-1

Published simultaneously in Canada by Beaverbooks, Ltd.
195 Allstate Parkway, Valleywood Business Park
Markham, Ontario L3R 4T8 Canada

I dedicate this book to all skiers everywhere, no matter how insane you are.

I also dedicate a special tribute to Don and Marvin Gainer, the Miller Twins, and Paul Webster, who took me skiing for my very first time.

On a day when the wind chill factor was 35 degrees *below* zero, they took me to the top of Mammoth Mountain, to the run called Climax. Then they waved good-bye and told me they would see me at the bottom. When I got there, they refused to ski with me because they said my snow-covered appearance embarrassed them.

They taught me that I can do anything.

They taught me that I can be a real skier.

They taught me the meaning of total terror.

Guys, I'll get even with you someday!

Gary Patterson

I've gotten a preview of what heaven must be like, and for that I thank the owners and staff of Mountain High, Goldmine, Snow Summit, Mammoth Mountain, and Snowmass. Surely their fun and atmosphere will be duplicated in paradise.

There are people whose knowledge and kindness have made even heaven better, so here is my chance to say thank you at last to them:

Two extraordinary coaches: that make-you-feel-good man, Tom Kelly, who knows everything about skiing; and Bob Takano, who knows everything about weightlifting.

Craig Reynolds, his wonderful deck, and everyone at Ski and Sports West.

Michelle Dowling and Pam Murphy, who know how to keep things in perspective except for an entertaining 5 percent of the time.

And Eric Chevasson, who knows the two quickest words in the English language.

Wina Sturgeon

CONTENTS

1. THE COMPLEAT SKIER 6
2. BEFORE THE FIRST FLAKE 14
3. THE MADNESS BEGINS 26
4. SURVIVAL ON THE SLOPES 40
5. CITIZENS OF THE SLOPES 46
6. HAZARDS OF THE SLOPES 58
7. MORE CITIZENS OF THE SLOPES 76
8. INTO THE NIGHT 94

1
THE COMPLEAT SKIER

Skiing is not just a sport, it is a state of mind. Skiers must hold this state of mind through spring, summer, and fall, while they wait for the slopes to turn white again.

When the obsession with skiing gets to be too much, you can find yourself getting out old brochures and rereading maps with all the check marks indicating bars you've passed out in. You go through ski magazines over and over until they look like they came from a dentist's office. You go to local sporting goods stores and beg the clerks to let you look at the ski equipment stored in the back room until the Annual August Sale. When walking to and from the train or parking lot you treat fellow pedestrians as if they were gates or (Heaven help you) moguls, zipping around and over them in a hunched position and holding imaginary ski poles. You keep up a pathetic one-way correspondence with slopeside condo owners.

FIRST FLAKE

When compleat skiers get together on a summer evening, you can often overhear them talking shop. They constantly debate over what sandwich construction of which synthetic materials is superior for each type of a vast variety of snow consistencies and degrees of slope. They can reach ludicrous depths of comparisons for ski boots, sweaters, jackets, goggles, hats, bindings, car racks, ski wax, gloves, pants, bibs—you name it.

They will buy every ski magazine that comes out, haunt ski shops, and sleep with their new boots. They will forget their jobs, neglect their families, and hock their homes to get money to ski. They will judge people by their Nastar medals. They will have no idea who the Vice-President is, but can name every member on the U.S. Ski Team since 1972.

THE COMPLEAT SKIER

Compleat skiers are a breed apart. They part from their money, they part from their comfort, they part from their other parts, and end up in casts. But in return, they learn things that flatlanders could never comprehend:

- a strange red spot on the snow does not confuse this breed—they can instantly indentify the level-ten fall required to burst a bota bag on snow.

- the triumph of willpower that comes from controlling your bladder as you bounce over the moguls, wishing beer had never been invented.

- the ability to crowd 82 party animals into a one-bedroom condo and still find a place to sleep.

- the knowledge of trajectory that enables you to click your skis together while on a lift so that the snow falls accurately on the heads of skiers below.

———————————

There is a hopelessness to the life of a skier, however. What other sport enthusiast would spend hundreds of dollars on special clothing and equipment, thousands on plane fares and accommodations, and twenty-odd bucks for a lift ticket—all for the privilege of falling down a mountain over and over again?

Who else would leave the warmth of their winter bed before the sun is up, travel for hours over hazardously slick and snow-covered roads, encase their feet in agonizingly torturous boots which force them to walk in a position that carries the torture up into their calves, and wait in line for a minimum of 20 minutes (and most likely an hour), just to dangle from an ice-encrusted chair that will stop halfway up the hill, and there freeze nearly to death while watching other people ski below them?

Who else will spend the whole winter relearning the painful lessons they forgot over the summer, just to have the season end, and go through the same process again and again, year after year?

You wonder how anyone could become addicted to such a sport. Is there really something transcendent about screaming down a mountain trail, barely avoiding trees and rocks, recklessly flying over mounds of snow and across bottomless crevasses, and dodging other hapless maniacs-on-skis that constantly cross your path? The compleat skier will tell you that it is so.

The compleat skier will never change. By the time he or she is too old to endure another ski season—somewhere around 33 years old—the compleat skier will have realized that fortunes have been squandered, that the knees have been trashed for good, and that imagination has taken over where memory fears to tread. The only words the compleat skier can understand are "What comes after excess?"

2
BEFORE THE FIRST FLAKE

Before the ski season formally begins, there are certain rituals in which every skier participates. There is the Annual August Ski Sale where you inevitably find the same skis you just had to buy midway through last season now $150 cheaper. You'll also find last year's experimental bindings that don't work; ski pants that fit perfectly except in the waist, hips, thighs, and knees; and three racks of fantastic sweater bargains, all in sizes 3, 4, and 5.

You also have resolved to be in better shape than last year, so you begin a quest for the perfect ski training regimen. The following few pages should get you started on the right track.

SKI SALE

THE SKI DECK

Some people hope to get a head start on the season by taking lessons on a ski deck. A ski deck is a revolving treadmill made of carpet. It will teach you how to ski on any mountain, as long as it's covered with carpet.

You'll learn a lot from the ski deck. You'll learn how to put your skis on while lying down, how to untangle them from your crumpled body, and how to untangle them from other people's crumpled bodies. These are the fundamental lessons everyone who skis should learn.

SUMMER SKIING

SHAPING UP

Many skiers believe that they need to get into shape before the ski season begins. They train their cardiovascular system for high altitudes. They train their muscles to endure hour after hour of skiing long mountain trails. They lift weights and run and stretch and ride their bikes. They even neglect their social life so they can be in shape to take full advantage of their expensive ski trip.

Funny thing, though. When they get to the ski resort, they find all that training was a waste of time. They spend only about 20 minutes a day skiing. The rest of the time is spent waiting in lift lines.

SNOW JOB

Skiers can become very cranky waiting for the first decent snowfall of the season as well as getting through to the recorded snow report.

It doesn't to take long for skiers to learn that the next biggest lie after "The check is in the mail," *is* the recorded snow report.

What you should do is call the mountain and ask for the rental shop or the snack bar or the lift maintenance shack. Anyone who answers will be an overworked and underpaid employee. This person will not *want* any more skiers on the hill. More skiers mean more curses from people who have discovered that the promised three foot base of packed powder is really three inches of soft slush. That's why this person will tell you the truth.

PRE-SKI BLUES

THE COST OF SKIING

We all know that skiing can be an expensive sport. But it's not because of the lift ticket or the tank of gas or the indigestion pills you need after the lodge lunch of canned nacho cheese sauce over stale tortilla chips.

Skiing is expensive because each time you go you have to replace a bent pole, a lost glove, ripped ski pants, the scarf you left at home, or the bottoms of your skies.

OUT OF CONTROL

LEARNING TO SKI

For those new to the slopes, a group lesson is the best way to learn. You learn humiliation. You learn despair. You learn that you are not on speaking terms with your muscles.

You forget every bit of compassion you ever had and begin praying that someone else falls before you do. You feel glad when it happens.

You wonder if the problems could be your skis. You wonder if you look as silly as all the rest of these clowns. You wonder if you will ever be able to come to a stop without falling down.

It doesn't matter. After the lesson, you will go to the bar. You will then discover exactly why so many people love skiing.

GROUP LESSON

3

THE MADNESS BEGINS

There comes a time when you don't need the snow reports to *know* that the hills or mountains are covered with snow. The miles of treacherous travel are nothing compared to the sight of miles of snow. There are miles of cars ahead of you as you slowly creep ever nearer the ski area parking lot. The weeks of waiting are nearly over. Hark! In the distance, you can hear the familiar mating sounds of the snow bunny: "Single!" Nirvana.

THE MOST DANGEROUS PART

There are three things you need to know about riding the chair lift:

1. getting on
2. staying on
3. getting off

Actually, you only have to worry about #2, since it's the only one where your very life is at stake.

A LONG WAY DOWN

It helps to remember the following things:

- Don't look down.
- The lift chair is very sturdy. You can grip it as tightly as you can. And you should.
- If the person next to you falls, don't be a hero.
- Don't look backward.
- More people die in cars than on chair lifts. Forget the fact that more people travel by car than chair lift.
- Don't even look up.
- Ski lifts are checked for efficient operation *at least* once a year.

TRUE FEAR

THE RULES OF LIFT DROPPING

The principles of dropping something from the lift are as follows:

1. Anything accidentally dropped from a chair lift falls either on the steepest part of the hill—where even the ski patrol fears to go—or it lands in unpacked, shoulder-high snow.

2. If it's rented, it's gone; if it's yours, it's damaged beyond hope of repair. If it's an article of clothing, it's in the next county, blowin' in the wind.

3. If you lose two of the same articles, you will only recover one of them.

DESPAIR

THE MOST DANGEROUS PART, PART II

Getting on the lift is no problem. You only have to sit down before the chair hits you in the back of the knee and topples you over.

Getting off the lift is no problem. You only have to stand up and move away before the chair hits you in the rear end and knocks you over.

Looking down while riding the lift *is* a problem. If you're like the average skier, it's not the fear of heights that scares you. It's the knowledge that you have to *ski* those icy cliffs below in order to get back to your car.

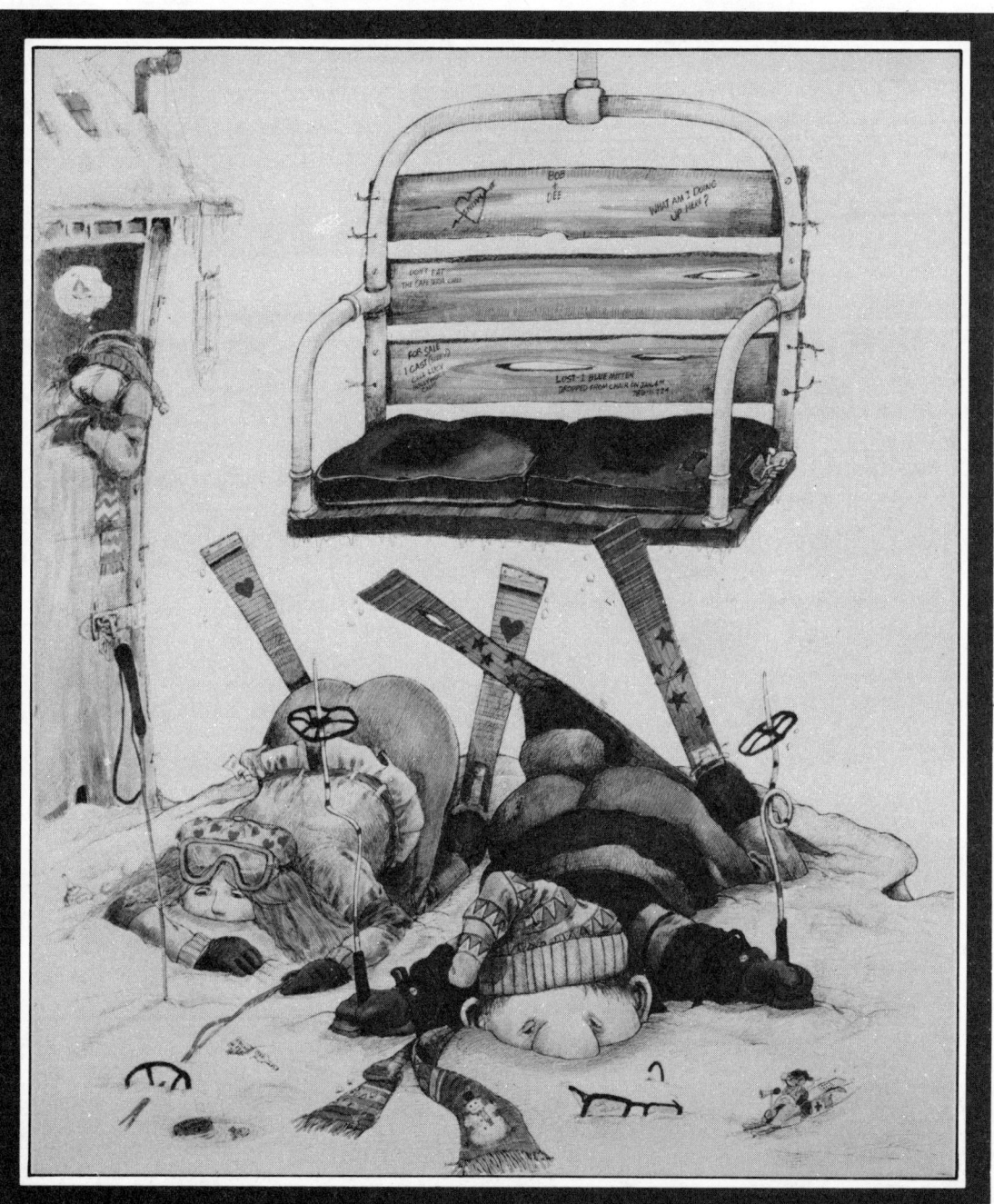

THE LIFT

THE T-BAR

The chair lift is not the only way to ride up the mountain. Many ski areas have T-bars. A T-bar tows clinging skiers up an icy track, giving them some experience in having their legs go out from under them even before they start skiing.

Most T-bars pull two people at a time. Riders are evenly matched: the rear end of one rider evenly matches the knees of the other in height. The bar gets the short one in the back and the tall one in the calves. Neither can ever manage the Olympic balancing skills required. Both fall off halfway up the hill.

This has led to a new winter sport: T-bar bowling. Spectators place bets on how many clinging skiers will be knocked down by sliders before they come to a stop.

T-BAR

ANOTHER SNOW JOB: TRAIL MAPS

Every ski area has a trail map. The trail map shows the mountain, the runs, the names of the runs, and the suggested skiing ability. The symbols used are a green circle for *easiest*, a blue square for *intermediate*, and a black diamond for *most difficult*.

Trail maps are not legally bound to Truth in Advertising laws. This should tell you something. However, as a general rule of thumb, you can rely on a trail map to tell you where the lifts are, where the restroom is, and where the parking lot can be found.

The easiest trails are the most difficult because so many skiers use them. You usually don't even need a sign to find these trails—just look for massive pile-ups.

EASY DECISION

Accuracy of Trail Symbols

If the mountain is frequented by risk-taking hotdoggers, the trail map will show true mountain macho by seriously understating the difficulty of the runs. *Easiest* will be like skiing down the leaning Tower of Pisa. *Intermediate* will be like skiing down the Grand Canyon. *Most difficult* will be like dropping out of an airplane.

If the mountain is frequented by colddoggers who only *think* they're hot, the trail map will stroke their egos. Green circle runs will be flat. Blue square runs will be flat. Black diamond runs will be steep enough so that a beach ball will roll all the way to the bottom, provided it has a tailwind.

What Trail Maps Never Tell You

Trail maps aren't designed to tell you anything about terrain, snow conditions, or weather. A perfectly innocuous little run may be covered with neck-high moguls made of solid ice. Perhaps the trees have grown a few feet wider since the map was drawn, and what was once a series of slalom-like gates is now a gauntlet of swinging doors. Those challenging ski jumps may be affected by vicious updrafts or downdrafts, which leave you somewhere not indicated on the map.

The time of day may affect your passage through a wooded area: in the morning, plenty of light; in the afternoon, so dark you can't see past your goggles. Or, on bitter cold mornings, the trails are a sheet of ice as hard as concrete.

Of course, it's impossible for the map to warn you that the group ahead of you, having partied all morning, is strewn all over the trail in the worst conceivable places.

4
SURVIVAL ON THE SLOPES

Many people think skiers ski for the sheer exhilaration of it. This is not the case. A large part of the thrill of skiing is the gamble: what are the chances of making it off the mountain alive?

To increase the odds, the next few pages include a basic skier's survival manual.

SURVIVAL ON THE SLOPES

RULES OF SURVIVAL, PART I

The **KEY** Rule: Any key in your pocket will be lost no matter how tightly your pocket is closed.

The **RULE OF THUMB**: Once you hurt your thumb, you will keep on hurting your thumb by falling on it, sitting on it, or skiing on it, even if you have never hurt your thumb before in your entire life.

The **OVERALL** Rule: No matter how good you look in stretch pants, the only thing that will keep you warm are those horrible bib overalls. Bib overalls are also so slippery that if you fall while wearing them, you will slide all the way to the parking lot.

RULES OF SURVIVAL, PART II

Sometimes survival means knowing when to keep your mouth shut, especially during the après ski brag session when your ski buddy is doing the bragging and that buddy is your only ride home. So, for survival's sake:

- If your friend brags about skiing outrageous moguls, don't point out that they were really only wind ripples.

- When your buddy impresses everyone with tales about skiing in a blizzard white out, don't mention that he was really skiing through the snow-making guns.

- When your bleary-eyed pal brags about not making it home until dawn last night, don't tell anyone that the reason was because he couldn't find his car.

SURVIVAL PREPARATION

The basic maxim of survival is *be prepared*. Being prepared may not help you change the situation, but it will help you know what to expect. For example:

- When you unbuckle your boots before getting on the chair lift, you will spend the entire ride wondering if the weight of your ski is going to pull your boot off.

- Your worst fall of the day will be caused by the cord from your cassette-player earphones tangling with your skis.

- If you haven't seen your ski buddy for a while and the loudspeaker asks you to report to the ski patrol office, you are not going to get good news.

SURVIVAL EXCUSE FOR THOSE WHO PREFER TO SIT IN THE LODGE ALL DAY

"If mankind were meant to ski, we would have been born with 200 cm feet."

No one will take this excuse seriously unless you say it with the required haughty air. After all, real wimps aren't arrogant.

5
CITIZENS OF THE SLOPES

PICKING A SKI BUDDY

It is essential that a skier have a ski buddy. You need *someone* who can watch your skis while you go to the bathroom. And *someone* has to drive the car back after you break your leg.

Choosing a ski buddy is both an art and a science. The best one is someone who owns a ski area. It eliminates buying lift tickets and waiting in line. Next best is someone who owns a helicopter with a pilot who can land in untracked powder. This buddy is less desirable only because après ski is somewhat limited in a helicopter and there's never a hot tub when you want one.

However, finding these two types of ski buddies is difficult. It becomes more difficult the less you look like Christie Brinkley or Mel Gibson. That means you may have to settle for pals with less material, but still valuable, attributes.

SKI BUDDY

People to Avoid

Do not go skiing with anyone who thinks a hot dog is a type of skier. To test a potential ski buddy before you actually plan a trip, ask yourself the following questions:

- Is this person likely to yell "Wimp, wimp, wimp!" at me if I refuse to ski down anything with less than the vertical slope of the Eiffel Tower?

- Is this person the kind to hold me in contempt if I suddenly remember an urgent phone call that requires my immediate presence in the lodge for the next two hours?

- Will this person laugh if it takes the ski patrol to pry my fingers from the chair lift?

If the answer to any of these questions is yes, find yourself another person to ski with.

HOT DOGGER

PICKING A SKI BUDDY: PART II

Remember that what falls on the mountains also falls on the roads. That's why it helps to have a ski buddy who can put on chains and *doesn't mind doing it!* On a blizzardy day, this person can also quickly clear a fortune by stopping near the "chains required" sign and charging $15 to chain up tires for the dummies who never learned how to do it themselves. You can both have a great time later in the lodge, when the blizzard closes the lifts.

Note: A person who can recognize the sound of a chain winding around an axle is also valuable to have on hand, as is a person who can unwind a chain from around an axle.

SKI CAR

THE SKI INSTRUCTOR

Ski instructors are the rock stars of the mountain. They make everything they do seem easy. Some people think ski instructors have nerves of steel, which is why they never mess up. This is simply not true! Their hair is made of steel, which is why their hair never gets messed up.

There certainly is a mystique about ski instructors that they are loathe to explain away. Let us examine some of these mythical aspects of the ski instructor.

SKI INSTRUCTOR

The Mystique, Part I

SKI INSTRUCTORS NEVER PICK UP ANYTHING THEY DROP. True. There are two reasons for this. The first is arrogance. A ski instructor doesn't *have* to pick up anything.

The second reason is physical limitation. In those tight pants, a ski instructor can't bend over to pick up anything!

The Mystique, Part II

SKI INSTRUCTORS SKI DANGEROUS PEAKS WHICH MORTAL SKIERS AVOID. False. This is not because the ski instructor is afraid. Ski instructors can ski these dangerous peaks quite well. It's just that, since there are no mortal skiers there to be impressed, the ski instructor sees no reason to ski them.

The Mystique, Part III

SKI INSTRUCTORS ARE GOD'S GIFT TO WOMEN. Wrong! A gift is something you can keep. On second thought, if you are very, very rich, you can probably keep a ski instructor.

The Mystique, Part IV

SKI INSTRUCTORS ARE SUPPOSED TO TEACH YOU TO SKI. No, no, no! Ski instructors are paid to lean back on their poles and look good. They're supposed to smile kindly when you fall, instead of wailing with laughter till the tears freeze on their cheeks. At their best, they will encourage you to take off down the mountain heedless of the hideous steepness or murderous moguls, in spite of their inherent love for humanity.

It takes incredible self-discipline to be a ski instructor. Don't expect miracles!

6
HAZARDS OF THE SLOPES

QUESTIONS OFTEN ASKED AT THE UNLOADING ZONE

- How did I let my boyfriend talk me into this?
- Why does that sign say, 'There *is* no easy way down?'
- Why is there nobody else up here and no one coming up on the lift?
- How can I stand up when my legs won't stop shaking?
- Can't I just stay on and go back down?

ANXIETY ATTACK

GETTING COURAGE

Standing on the edge of a steep run, trying to get the nerve to start, is a paralyzing experience. There are two ways to overcome top-of-the-run cowardice:

1. Shut your eyes, start skiing, and accept the fact that you are about to take a class-10 eggbeater fall. You can feel good knowing that you are about to give some ski patroller something to talk about for the rest of the season.

2. Wait a bit longer. Soon you will have to go to the bathroom. A full bladder overcomes petrified fear every single time.

PROCRASTINATION

MORE ON MOGULS

Moguls are pimples on the mountain of progress. Moguls will break your heart, your ego, and, worse, your skis.

Moguls aren't there to get *you* in particular. Moguls don't discriminate. They are there to get *everyone*.

Occasionally, you will see a skier pumping away through the mogul field with grace and ease. Don't let this get you down. This is a professional stunt person who is paid $2,000 a day by the resort manager to create the illusion that the moguls can actually be skied.

ALL DRESSED UP AND NOWHERE TO GO

SPEED DOES NOT KILL

It's a common belief among top skiers that speed is the essential factor that prevents them from falling. The trick is to reach a speed of 64 feet per second (approximately 135 mph) while remaining on your skis. The scientific term for this is *terminal velocity*. You can't go any faster, even if you fell.

RELIGION ON THE SLOPES

There are no athiests on a black diamond run.

BLACK DIAMOND RUN

SKIER'S PRAYER

Now I stand
On the mountaintop
It's 20 below zero
And the wind won't stop
My body's freezing
And shaking with fear
It's a long way down
Lord, I hope you're near.
If you are listening
And can hear this poem
Get me outta here
I wanna go home!

Gary Patterson

SKIER'S PRAYER

FALLING

When you fall, the first thing you do is look around to see if anyone witnessed your humiliation. When you fall and require the ski patrol to take you down the mountain, remember one thing: the ride on the sled is free. The mask to cover your face is $100.

There are many categories of falls. Here are a few of the major ones:

- Falls where you slide all the way to the bottom, but your skis stay on top.

- Falls where you are wearing old-fashioned leashes, so your ski continuously clonks you about the head and body as you barrel down the hill.

- Falls where you end up so pretzeled and stripped of gear that people ask you where your parachute is.

- Falls where you can do nothing but lie there going, *"Uhhhhhh . . . uhhhhhh . . . uhhhhhh,"* while 17 people gather around demanding an immediate answer to the question "Are you all right?"

- Falls that include other people, trees, and small buildings. These are not reported as avalanches. But they should be.

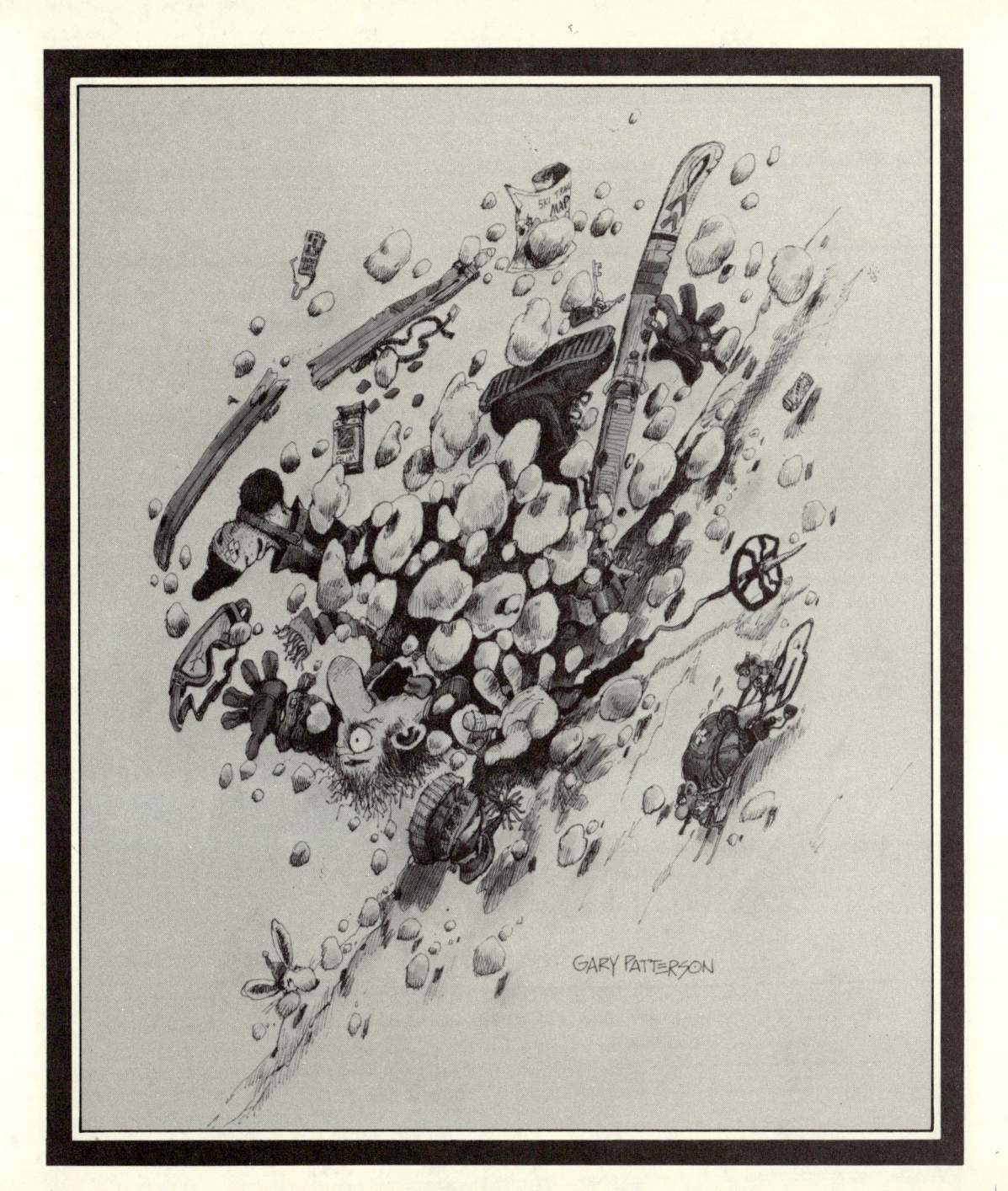

AVALANCHE

THE AGONY OF DE FEET

Modern technology has really progressed. In medieval times, it took a well-equipped dungeon to cause ultimate agony. Today we can do it with a simple plastic shoe called the ski boot.

The first stage is a cramp in your foot. This is psychologically timed so that it happens on the lift, the only place on the mountain where you can't loosen the boot to ease the pain.

Next comes an exploding ball of agony in the ball of your foot. After that, the boots seem to shrink, squashing the edges of your feet.

At this point, your nerve endings usually pass the pain threshold and your feet go numb. You continue to ski, thinking that's the end of it. But wait.

A week later, just as your feet begin to feel normal again, you notice your big toenails turning black. Three days later, they fall off, leaving you unable to wear shoes for the next two months.

GARY PATTERSON

EGO RUNS

Any run that goes under the chair lift, is steep, difficult, treacherous, and ungroomed. These trails are known as *ego runs*.

The term is actually a bit of subtle sarcasm. You usually ski them by accident, as the skiers riding above you whistle and jeer while you tear recklessly down the mountain.

IN FULL CONTROL

SKIING ON THE ROCKS

Rock skis are your other skis, the ones you use when the mountain is bare, like on the first day the lifts open or during so-called "spring" skiing (so-called because it's like skiing in a mountain spring).

Rock skis are made, not bought. You make them because you believed the snow report. You make them by trying that great-looking trail that no one else seemed to be using. You make them by lending your good skis to a friend.

Rock skis allow you a great degree of freedom because you don't have to worry when skiing through trees or the backcountry. The bottoms are so gouged and scraped and pockmarked that they are more like skinny snowshoes than skis.

And who ever went fast enough to get hurt on a pair of snowshoes?

ON THE ROCKS

7
MORE CITIZENS OF THE SLOPES

THE RECREATIONAL RACER

Racing adds a new dimension to the sport of skiing—bankruptcy. Racers will spend any amount of money to take a few seconds off their time. They will buy any gadget, travel thousands of miles for special coaching, and spend hours tuning and waxing their skis before each race.

Real racers usually have a collection of trophies. Every one of the trophies has the same plastic figure of a skier who looks nothing like a racer. If you add it all up, each trophy has cost approximately $13,469, not counting tax.

SKI RACER

THE *SERIOUS* RECREATIONAL RACER

Races can be medal races, where you may win a gold, silver, or bronze, depending on whether you skied down the course, walked down the course, or stopped and had lunch on the course.

Races can also be trophy races, where awards are given for first, second, and third place. Part of winning a trophy race is psyching out your opponents. Here are some suggestions for how to do it right:

- Ask other racers in your class if they have ever thought about taking lessons.

- Tell other racers that you used to have equipment like theirs—the week you start skiing.

- Wait until the starter is counting a racer down, then yell out, "Your pants are unzipped!"

- Sneak into other racers' condos late at night and fill their boots with mashed potatoes.

SKI BUNNY

Usually seen waiting for someone to buy her a drink, the ski bunny has no money to buy one for herself. She spent it all at her local ski shop. It took her three weeks to find the perfect ski outfit in just the right colors (cost: $400). It made her behind look like two moguls side-by-side. She searched seven shopping malls for the right ski sweater to match (cost: $150). It makes her mole hills look like mountains. She tried on 100 different pairs of *aprés* ski boots before finding a pair that made her size nines look like tiny powder puffs (cost: $95).

It took her three minutes to pick out skis, bindings, and poles, which she bought used for $35. That's okay. They're only props, anyway. She has no intention of actually going skiing.

SKI BUNNY

NEUROSES ON THE SLOPES

The self-conscious skiier is positive that everyone within ten miles of the resort saw him fall and is now watching him slink down the mountain. Camera crews will be there soon to tape it for film at 11. Do you think this person will get to the bottom, put on his skis, and try again on an easier hill? No, no, no.

He will slip into the bar, have two LA beers, and pull his collar up around his face so no one recognizes him. Then, he'll go out and hide in the car until his clothes are completely dry so he can return his rental equipment without catching grief from the guys in the shop.

GARY PATTERSON

RACE CAMP

Race camp is where the serious recreational ski racer goes because it feels so good to wear a racing bib all week.

You will make many friends at race camp. These friendships will last, unless a friend who was slower at the beginning of the week becomes faster than you by the end of the week.

There is usually a big race on the last day of race camp, and at the start of the week, all campers sign up for it knowing they'll have an edge. That's before they discover that a daily 17-hour routine of stretching and exercise, learning and practicing countless techniques, and intensive gate training will have so flogged their muscles that they can be beaten by a snow-plowing, middle-aged stockbroker who decided to try the race because it looked like fun.

RACE CAMP

THE APRES SKI LODGE

The lodge is the place where people go to partake of that euphemism known as *après ski*. It's where skiers go to relax, while others are outside combing the snow for their missing car keys, or combing the snow for their missing friends, or stealing the après skiers' skis.

Two categories of people can be found at the lodge: mountain employees and skiers.

Mountain employees are all victims of "T. K.'s rule of catch-22." They loved skiing so much that they left the flatlands and started working for the ski industry just to find that they have no time left for skiing. This dilemma has been a factor in developing a certain cynical attitude toward skiers on the part of the mountain employee.

THE LODGE

Lodge Lounge Lizards

Lounge lizards usually travel as a group of ski buddies who come in, sit down, make a lot of noise, and tell rude jokes to the waitress.

There are four major subdivisions usually seen within these groups:

THE NEVER-EVER. This person has never-ever been skiing before. After his buddies took him up to the top and left him, he will never-ever go skiing again.

Usually seen white-faced and trembling.

THE WANNABE. This person will try anything once. Once is all he gets. Then ski patrol takes him down the mountain on a sled.

Usually seen in a cast.

THE GIM (GOSH, I'M GOOD). Thinks he is headed for the U.S. Ski Team because he can make it down the bunny run standing up.

Usually seen with mouth flapping.

THE IMNBGBIOACAPAASP. (I May Not Be Good, But I Own a Condo, a Porsche, and a Season Pass).

Not often seen on snow. Usually seen on the make.

NEVER-EVER

The Drinker

    This type begins his après ski before putting on his boots. He rents a locker and fills it with bota bags, because he feels more secure when he's *really* holding his liquor. He doesn't know that he's riding the lift single, because after his first run he's already seeing double.

    Once inside the lodge, he has a dim impression that he's no longer skiing. After a few more drinks, the bartender tells him he's had enough and that he should sleep it off. He does, under the table. Nobody notices he's there until his breath melts someone's shoes.

ANTI-FREEZE

The *Après Ski* Bum

This person has had a hard day. The first thing he did was to fall over and hug the snow—in the lift line. It was only on the chair that he remembered his terror of heights. He fell getting off the lift, and the next three chairs dumped their occupants on him. When he tried to get up, his skis kept zipping out from under him. He had to slither down the lift ramp so that some pimply-faced kid could pull him up. It took four tries. When he started down the trail, he couldn't make the first turn, and he went off into the trees. He spent the rest of the day looking for his left ski. His fingers are frostbitten. His eyelids are sunburned. He is in pain.

In the lodge, a blonde in pink stretch pants says hello. He buys her a drink. She invites him to the Jacuzzi where she's staying. They get up to leave, and he wishes he weren't leaving tonight. Skiing is great! It's fantastic! He can't wait to come back!

HOW TO TALK LIKE A SKIER

You can't be a real skier unless you know how to talk like one. As a skier, your conversations should consist of the following topics:

- injuries you have had
- falls you have taken
- falls you have seen other people take
- pain you have suffered
- doctors' bills you have paid
- places you have skied before and injuries you had there, falls you had, falls you saw, and so on.

8

INTO THE NIGHT

APRES *APRES SKI*

When you leave the lodge, your education as a skier will truly reach new depths. You will learn how to find your condo when your friends disappear with the car, the keys, and the person you recently saw them talking to.

You will learn that the last one in the condo has to climb over the most people to find a bed.

You will find out that no matter how late you come in, the noisiest person in your group won't come back until you are asleep.

You will discover that there is something about a ski mountain that amplifies snoring.

You will realize that, if eight skiers can share a bathroom and survive, world peace *is* possible.

SKI LOVER